Scholastic BookFiles

A READING

Out of the Dust

by Karen Hesse

Mary Varilla Jones

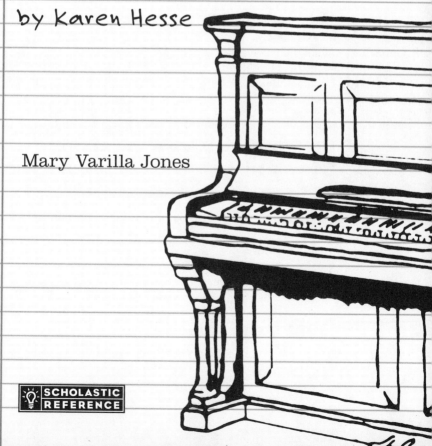

SCHOLASTIC
REFERENCE

Copyright © 2004 by Scholastic Inc.
Interview © 2004 by Karen Hesse
Recipe on p. 58 © 2004 Catherine M. Murphy

All rights reserved. Published by Scholastic Inc.

SCHOLASTIC, SCHOLASTIC REFERENCE, SCHOLASTIC BOOKFILES, and associated logos are trademarks and/or registered trademarks of Scholastic Inc.

No part of this publication may be reproduced, or stored in a retrieval system, or transmitted in any form or by any means, electronic, mechanical, photocopying, recording, or otherwise, without written permission of the publisher. For information regarding permission, write to Scholastic Inc., Attention: Permissions Department, 557 Broadway, New York, NY 10012.

0-439-53834-3

10 9 8 7 6 5 4 3 2 1   04 05 06 07 08

Composition by Brad Walrod/High Text Graphics, Inc.
Cover and interior design by Red Herring Design

Printed in the U.S.A.   23
First printing, June 2004

Contents

About Karen Hesse

"I feel so fortunate that I have a job that encourages me to read and discover new things."

—Karen Hesse

Karen Hesse was not a happy, carefree kid. She was always upset about something. "My mother tells me there never was a more miserable child," Hesse admits.

How does a child like that turn into a famous, award-winning author? Karen Hesse is as unique and colorful as the characters in her books.

Karen Hesse was born on August 29, 1952, in Baltimore, Maryland. Growing up, she had a very active imagination. Hesse would sometimes imagine things that were so scary she had trouble sleeping at night. When she went shopping with her mother as a young child, she would see the clothes on the racks reaching for her. Even dinner could sometimes upset Karen. She hated Chinese food so much that she would whine all the way through family dinners at Mee Jon Lows, a local Chinese restaurant. (She learned to like Chinese food as an adult, though!)

There were happy times, too. Hesse enjoyed writing poetry and playing with the many kids who lived in her neighborhood. She especially loved spending time with her big brother, Mark. When she wanted time alone, Hesse would curl up with a good book— make that *climb* up with a good book. Hesse would walk out her back door, book in hand, and climb an apple tree. "There, cradled in the boughs of the tree, I spent hours reading. Often my bony bottom would go numb, but I loved it up there so much, I ignored the discomfort."

Hesse remembers being awkward as a child, with "long skinny legs, buckteeth, tons of freckles, enormous green eyes, and a mop of brown curls. I seemed to be all angles and bones through elementary school." She didn't like big groups and didn't need to be the center of attention. "As a child, I usually faded into the background. I liked being unnoticed."

When her stepsister entered her life, things changed for Hesse. Her stepsister was beautiful and became a professional dancer while still in high school. Hesse was jealous. She decided to try acting so people would notice her, too. Her high school drama teacher was impressed with her talent and helped Hesse get into the theater program at Towson State College in Maryland.

"So why am I a writer and not an actress?" Hesse has asked. "One day, as I prepared to run lights for a student production in the studio theater, a young man came up to the light booth. A mutual friend introduced us. It was love at first sight. For both of us."

Hesse left school and was married in 1971. She later finished her college education at the University of Maryland. She spent some of her free time at the school writing poetry and giving poetry readings. She also held many kinds of jobs. She worked in a pizza bagel shop, as a nanny, and in a library at her university. The library work was her favorite. "Working in a library, well, I loved that the way I love chocolate pudding. It was truly that good," Hesse has shared.

From that point on, almost all of Hesse's jobs had something to do with reading. She worked as a proofreader, as an advertising secretary at a magazine, and as a typesetter. It was while working with children's books as a typesetter that she first began to believe that she could become a children's-book author.

In 1976, Hesse and her husband, Randy, settled in Vermont. There they raised their two daughters, Kate and Rachel. Hesse loved being a mom, but she never lost her interest in writing for children. In fact, reading to her young daughters made her want to write even more.

Becoming an author wasn't easy. Hesse began writing books for children in 1980, but she had trouble finding a publisher. "There were nine years when I submitted work and received not one acceptance. I think a less stubborn person would've given up!" she has admitted. But Hesse didn't give up. Her first book, *Wish on a Unicorn*, was published in 1991. Since then, she has published more than a dozen books and received many awards. With such great success, Karen Hesse is certainly not miserable anymore!

"But how could I re-create the dust bowl? I was born in 1952, in Baltimore, Maryland. What did I know from dust?"

—Karen Hesse, excerpt from Newbery acceptance speech, June 27, 1998

In 1993, Karen Hesse and her friend Liza Ketchum took a car trip to Colorado. On the way there, they traveled through Kansas. Hesse had never been to this part of the United States before. Seeing the Great Plains for the first time was an amazing experience for her. A tornado struck on her first day in Kansas. On her second day, she visited a town so small that it was never given a name. Hesse remembers that day: "The wind never stopped blowing there. It caressed our faces, it whispered in our ears. The grass moved like a corps of dancers. The colors were unlike any I had ever encountered on the East Coast or the West. And the sky and land went on to the horizon and beyond."

Hesse's visit to Kansas stayed with her. Three years later, her memories of the Plains found a place in her writing. Hesse was working on her picture book, *Come On, Rain!* She shared her work with her writing group and asked them what they thought. The three authors who make up her writing group spoke honestly. They didn't understand why the character in her book wanted rain so much.

"I started thinking about times in this country when people really wanted it to rain. So I came back to the Dust Bowl," recalls Hesse. "Being the writer I am, when I started thinking about the Dust Bowl, I started researching. I became so fascinated by that period of history and the people living then that I put the picture book aside and began writing *Out of the Dust.*"

Hesse researched and researched and researched. She had never lived in Oklahoma or during the 1930s and wanted to make sure she had all the details just right. She read books about wheat farming. She read books about dust. She even contacted the Oklahoma Historical Society for help. "I saturated myself with those dusty, dirty, desperate times, and what I discovered thrilled me," Hesse has explained. Hesse's most useful discovery was the *Boise City News*, a newspaper published in the Oklahoma Panhandle in the 1930s.

As Hesse pored over the issues of the *Boise City News*, she was surprised by what she found. "The dust storms were only minor articles—what was going on there was life! There were concerts and plays and schools. . . . So I made Billie Jo connected to the arts, because I wanted the reader to understand that even if people were struggling under such harsh circumstances, they would find a way to keep joy in their lives."

Hesse has admitted she had personal reasons for making Billie Jo a poet and a pianist. "I'm both a poet and a musician—

although I'm not very good at either, I'm afraid!" Hesse enjoys music so much that she has said that if she weren't a writer, she'd be a musician. She'd love to conduct beautiful symphonies.

Hesse gave Billie Jo's character a love of music, but she decided to make Billie Jo's character face terrible tragedy, too. She is often asked whether the accident in *Out of the Dust* could have actually taken place. Could someone really confuse kerosene and water? "Yes. It happened often," Hesse has answered. "I based the accident on a series of articles appearing in the 1934 *Boise City News*. That particular family tragedy planted the seed for *Out of the Dust*, as much as the dust storms did."

Was all of the research and hard work worth it? You bet. *Out of the Dust* won many awards, including the John Newbery Medal, and helped make Karen Hesse a famous writer. But don't look for a sequel. Hesse has been asked to write sequels to many of her books, but has always said no. She finds creating brand-new characters and fresh stories more interesting.

An Interview with Karen Hesse

About *Out of the Dust*

◆ *Did you interview people who lived during the Dust Bowl when you were researching* Out of the Dust?

No. The intimate details of life in the Oklahoma Panhandle during the 1930s came almost exclusively from scouring reels and reels of newspaper on microfilm.

◆ *The entries in* Out of the Dust *are dated as if Billie Jo wrote them in a journal. Have you ever kept a journal?*

Yes.

◆ *You must have done a lot of research about plants and farming in order to write* Out of the Dust. *Your descriptions of the wheat crops, Ma's apple trees, and Mrs. Brown's cereus plant are wonderfully detailed! Have you tried gardening or farming yourself?*

My gardening skills leave a great deal to be desired. However, the germination of a tiny seed, its growth into a mature plant, fascinates me. Such a miracle. I watch my husband, who is the true gardener in the family. He tends the garden the way I tend the words in my books. He sees the plant weeds when I do not. I see the word weeds when others read right past them. So perhaps I am a gardener—my medium, though, is words and concepts rather than seeds and dirt.

About being a writer

◆ *What's the most challenging part of being a writer?*

Life places so many obstacles in the path of a writer. It is difficult to stay on task at times, particularly when the work is not going well. Or when something distracting turns my thoughts away from the computer. Perhaps my dog is ill, or my washing machine is overflowing, or a tragedy has unbalanced the nation. I must admit that many times I take care of those demands first and momentarily put my work aside. Or there are times when I want to simply engage in life, rather than taking the measure of every little detail that rushes past me and placing it in a brain file for later use in a book. Or I can get so wrapped up in my research that I don't know how to stop reading. Or I will saturate my brain with so much information but I don't know how to start writing. All of these challenges, and more, complicate the process of writing a book.

◆ *What's the best part?*

When I'm writing I feel more alive, more complete, than at any other time. When I'm writing I have a sense of everything being right in the world, even if terrible things are happening to the characters in my created world and terrible things are happening to people in the real world. Inside me everything is in place and functioning as it was meant to function. It's hard to describe. It's glorious to experience.

◆ *When you have finished writing one of your books, who gets to read it first?*

Let's talk instead about drafts rather than finished books. When I finish writing a draft, the first reader is determined by the kind of book I'm trying to write. For example, my daughter Rachel understands me well; she also understands children's literature. If I am taking risks, if I am creating a sort of high-wire act with a story, I will give an early draft to Rachel to see if I'm making any sense at all. My writing group also gets an early look. They often see the manuscript two or three times during the years of revisions. My editor, of course, reads the manuscript at several stages in its development, and my husband and my daughter Kate read the final drafts. If I need expert readers (and I often do), they read the manuscript in its earlier stages so that if I am heading down the wrong path they can correct me before I've invested too much time exploring a dead end.

◆ *Which do you enjoy more: doing research for a book or actually writing it?*

It's hard to say. Finding the resources feels much like going on a scavenger hunt. Tracking down references, holding them in my hands, diving into them . . . that is so rewarding, so satisfying, so much fun. Learning about my subject, becoming a Sunday-night expert in a wide array of new fields keeps me excited and engaged, though it makes me an odd dinner companion as I offer obscure little factoids whenever there is a lull in the conversation. However, when I'm writing and the writing is going well, ahhh, those are the best times, the golden times. I suppose, if I had to choose, it would be the actual writing I love the most.

◆ *Do you ever work on more than one book at a time?*

Yes. As one book is approaching final stage, another is usually in midstage revisions, another in early draft or late research, and another is a little seed, restless under the soil, waiting impatiently for conditions to be just right for germination.

◆ *Have you ever started writing a book and not finished it?*

Definitely. Though it doesn't happen often, I can reach the writing stage and find I don't care enough about the characters, or the book. No matter how many changes, the manuscript will never be of a quality my readers deserve. In the case of *Just Juice*, Juice was a secondary character in another, entirely different novel. I didn't feel that novel was strong enough and so I withdrew it from my publisher. However, Juice wouldn't be put off. Happily I made her the star of a spin-off show, and the resulting book justified every hour I'd spent on the original story.

♦ *Your book* A Light in the Storm *was made into a play through the Kennedy Center's Imagination Celebration on Tour program. What was it like to see one of your books performed onstage?*

It is thrilling to see the internal geography of your book, the characters, the setting, the plot, unfold externally on the stage. Dressed in its theatrical costume, the story is transformed into something beyond its original conception. It is very powerful, very moving for me as the author to see the product of my imagination brought to life.

♦ *Are there plans for any of your other books to be made into plays or movies?*

There has been much discussion, much negotiation, but no deal.

♦ *Your grandfather was supposed to be a passenger on the* Titanic *but he sold his ticket and took the next boat. That's an amazing story. Have you ever thought of writing about it?*

Yes, but I couldn't find my way into the story. The research led me to write *Letters from Rifka* instead.

General

♦ *If you had more free time, how would you spend it?*

Reading for pleasure.

◆ *You have said that if you were not a writer, you'd like to be a musician. What kind of music do you like? Do you play any instruments?*

I like many kinds of music: classical, jazz, folk, rock, blues. I sing in a chorus (my voice has a very narrow range but I LOVE to sing and blend my reedy alto with other voices). I play the piano and the recorder very poorly, but when I am engaged in making music the writer in me is disengaged, and it's delicious to have a vacation from her.

◆ *Apart from writing, what are you best at?*

I like to help people by hearing them, really hearing them. I'm best at being quietly present.

◆ *What are you bad at?*

Too many things to list.

Chapter Charter: Questions to Guide Your Reading

The following questions will help you think about the important parts of each chapter.

Winter 1934

- Why did Daddy name his daughter Billie Jo? How might Billie Jo's life be different if she were a boy?
- How does Billie Jo feel about Livie Killian's moving away? Have you ever had a friend move away? How did it feel?
- Do you think Billie Jo should be mad at Ma for not allowing her to miss school to play piano? Why or why not?
- How does Ma respond to Billie Jo's scores on the state test? Did you ever feel you deserved more praise from your family than you got?

Spring 1934

- What does Billie Jo do for comfort? Is there something you like to do when you're upset or want to relax?
- Why does Ma allow Billie Jo to play with Arley Wanderdale on the road?
- Have you ever performed in a concert or play or had people watch you play in a big game? How did it feel to have an audience?
- If you were Daddy, would you "give up on wheat"? Why does he decide to keep growing it?

Summer 1934

- Whose fault is the accident?
- Should Billie Jo forgive her father for leaving Ma to go drinking in Guymon?
- How does Billie Jo spend her birthday?
- Why does Billie Jo hide her injured hands from her father?
- Why does Daddy want to dig a pond now?

Autumn 1934

- Why can't Billie Jo stand to be in the same room with a piano anymore?
- How does Mad Dog treat Billie Jo? What would you say to Billie Jo if she were your friend?
- What kinds of paintings are shown at the art exhibit? Why do they mean so much to Billie Jo?

Winter 1935

- Billie Jo writes that Christmas without Ma and Franklin "wouldn't have been so bad, / if I'd just remembered the cranberry sauce." Does your family make any special foods for a holiday celebration? How would the holiday feel without them?
- In what ways is Billie Jo like her father? Who are you the most like in your family?
- Is it right for Miss Freeland to let Buddy Williams and his family stay at the school?
- After the Williamses' baby is born, Billie Jo feels she must "go away for a little while / and just walk off the feelings." What kinds of feelings do you think she's experiencing?
- Do you think Billie Jo deserved to win third place at the talent show?

Spring 1935

- How does Billie Jo feel about Mad Dog Craddock? How do you know?
- Why is Billie Jo upset with her father about the letter from Aunt Ellis? How would you feel if you were Billie Jo?
- Do you think Daddy is being a good father to Billie Jo? Why or why not?

Summer 1935

- If you were Billie Jo, would you have run away?
- How does Billie Jo's father compare with the man she meets in the boxcar of the train?
- Why do you think Billie Jo is able to call her father Daddy for the first time since her mother died?

Autumn 1935

- How do you know that Billie Jo has accepted Louise?
- Does anything on Billie Jo's Thanksgiving List surprise you?
- What do you think will happen to Billie Jo, Daddy, and Louise?

Plot: What's Happening?

"Hard times are about losing spirit,
and hope,
and what happens when dreams dry up."

—*Out of the Dust*

Out of the Dust tells the story of Billie Jo Kelby, a thirteen-year-old girl who lives on a family farm in Oklahoma. The story begins in winter 1934, a time when dust storms are destroying crops and making it difficult for families in Oklahoma and other southwestern states to earn enough to survive.

Even though her family is struggling, Billie Jo is full of hope. She is excited to find out that Ma is expecting a new baby. Then there's more happy news. Arley Wanderdale, a local musician and music teacher, asks her to play piano at the Palace Theatre. Billie Jo loves playing piano and wants to perform—even though her rival, Mad Dog Craddock, was asked to play, too. Billie Jo describes her performance, saying, "It's the best / I've ever felt, / playing hot piano. . . ." Billie Jo is thrilled when Ma gives her permission to travel with Arley Wanderdale to play piano during the summer.

Just when Billie Jo is finding happiness in her dusty world, her family is torn apart in a terrible tragedy. While making Daddy's coffee, Ma picks up a bucket that Daddy had placed next to the stove. Instead of water, the bucket holds kerosene, and a fire breaks out. Ma runs outside to tell Daddy. Billie Jo follows, then remembers the fiery bucket inside. She grabs it and throws the kerosene out the door, not realizing that Ma is standing there. Ma becomes a "column of fire." When Billie Jo tries to beat out the flames to save Ma, her hands are burned badly. Ma dies a few days later after giving birth to a son named Franklin.

As the weeks pass, Billie Jo and Daddy have difficulty adjusting. Arley Wanderdale encourages Billie Jo to play piano again. He invites her to play at a dance revue that his wife, Vera, is putting together. Billie Jo says she'll try.

Billie Jo practices on the school piano every day before and after class to prepare for a talent contest at the Palace Theatre. Her hard work is rewarded when she wins third place at the contest. Some contestants say the judges were only being kind to Billie Jo because of her injuries. But Billie Jo isn't bothered by what others have to say or by the pain she feels after playing with all her might. "I ignored the pain running up and down my arms, / I felt like I was part of something grand."

Arley asks Billie Jo to play in a show at the school. But when the time comes, Billie Jo's hands still hurt from her performance at the Palace and the show goes badly for her. She says, "I did play like a cripple at Arley's show, / not that Arley would ever say it." She doesn't think Arley will ask her to play again.

As the days pass, Billie Jo grows restless. She says her father and she "can't soothe each other." Billie Jo also notices that Daddy is developing spots on his skin like the ones that killed his father—skin cancer. Aunt Ellis writes and invites Billie Jo to live with her in Lubbock, Texas. This only adds to her troubles. Billie Jo doesn't want to go and is confused when her father says, "Let's wait and see."

Things keep going badly for the Kelbys. Daddy's wheat crops are poor and the family has little money. Billie Jo is invited to play piano at graduation, but when her turn comes she just stares at the keys and can't play. She is also troubled because her father won't see a doctor about his spots. "I think we're both turning to dust," she says.

As summer 1935 begins, Billie Jo is so filled with anger and sadness that she decides to stow away in the boxcar of a train heading west, "out of the dust." Two days into her journey, a man climbs into Billie Jo's boxcar. She gives him her day's biscuits and they share stories about their lives. Billie Jo says, "I told him about my father / and how the thing that scared us both the most / was being left alone. / . . . My father / stayed rooted, even with my tests and my temper, / even with the double sorrow of / his grief and my own, / he had kept a home / until I broke it."

Billie Jo drifts off to sleep. When she awakens, the man and all of her biscuits are gone. Billie Jo decides to get off the train in Flagstaff, Arizona, and calls Mr. Hardly so he can tell her father that she's coming home.

Daddy meets Billie Jo at the train station. As they walk home, he promises to go see Doc Rice. Billie Jo tells the reader that she is learning to forgive her father and herself for all that they have faced.

Doc Rice cuts the cancer out of Daddy's skin and examines Billie Jo's hands. He tells Billie Jo that ointment will help, but most of all she needs to use them.

Daddy's friend Louise comes to dinner. Louise stayed with Daddy while Billie Jo was away. Billie Jo admits, "I didn't intend to, but I liked her. . . ." A few weeks later, Daddy takes Louise to Ma and Franklin's grave to tell Ma his plan. He wants to marry Louise.

Louise helps Daddy get a second mule as an engagement gift. He will work the land with mules because the tractor is broken and there's no money to fix it. He's also going to plant different kinds of crops. He says that "you can stay in one place / and still grow."

Thinking about the plot

- Why does Billie Jo want to get "out of the dust"? What makes her decide to stay?
- How does Billie Jo's relationship with her father change during the novel?
- Do you think *Out of the Dust* has a happy ending? Why or why not?

"Dust
piles up like snow
across the prairie,
dunes leaning against fences,
mountains of dust pushing over barns."

—*Out of the Dust*

Out of the Dust is set in the Oklahoma Panhandle between January 1934 and December 1935. Overused land, endless days without rain, strong winds, and record high temperatures have led to violent dust storms there. The storms have blown away acres of topsoil, destroyed crops, and killed livestock. Gone are the plentiful fields of waist-high golden wheat that used to grow. The dust storms have become so bad that the places they strike—Oklahoma, Colorado, Texas, Kansas, and New Mexico— are nicknamed the Dust Bowl.

Place: Where are we?

Billie Jo Kelby lives on a farm in Cimarron County, Oklahoma. Cimarron County is a real place. So are Texhoma, Guymon, and the other towns described in *Out of the Dust*. Most of them can be found in the Oklahoma Panhandle. If you're not sure where the

Panhandle is, you can look at a map of Oklahoma. You'll see that the state looks something like a rectangle with a long, narrow strip attached to its top left side. That narrow strip is the Panhandle.

When you read *Out of the Dust*, you can imagine what it was like to live in the Oklahoma Panhandle in the mid-1930s. You can see, feel, and even taste the dust. Dust is always with Billie Jo. It covers her food and dinner table. It layers the floors and furniture of her home. Dust even blows into Billie Jo's school during an important test. "While we sat / taking our six-weeks test, / the wind rose / and the sand blew / right through the cracks in the schoolhouse wall. . . ."

Some of the dust storms are so bad that cars and trucks stop running and people get lost trying to find shelter. Billie Jo tells of one particularly frightening dust storm in the entry called "Blankets of Black." The storm she describes actually happened on April 14, 1935. One of the worst storms of the Dust Bowl, its date became known as Black Sunday.

Dust isn't the only hardship facing Oklahomans in the 1930s. Hungry jackrabbits and grasshoppers add to their troubles. They eat the few crops that do manage to grow.

Time: When does our story happen?

Out of the Dust begins in January 1934, in the middle of the Great Depression. The Great Depression started when the stock market crashed in October 1929 and continued throughout the

1930s. It was a time in United States history when wages were very low and many people had no work at all. People struggled to meet everyday needs.

Bountiful wheat crops protected Oklahoma farmers from the Great Depression at first. But after 1931, the wheat crops failed. The crops could not survive the dust storms and hailstorms. Families came upon hard times.

Like most families in the United States in the 1930s, Billie Jo's family is very poor. Karen Hesse helps us understand just how poor the Kelbys are through her descriptions of the family. Ma sews a nightie for the new baby out of a feed sack rather than softer, more expensive material. Billie Jo wears tattered clothes. "I slipped the coins into my sweater pocket, the pocket / without the hole. . . ."

The Kelbys have far worse troubles. Billie Jo's father is having a hard time earning money to pay the bills and keep his farm going. He is forced to take loans from the government in order to have enough money to plant more wheat. Sometimes Ma and Daddy quarrel over what to do. "Ma says, / 'Who pays the bills?' / 'No one right now,' Daddy says."

At this time, many families chose to leave the Dust Bowl in search of better lives. "And so they go, / fleeing the blowing dust, / fleeing the fields of brown-tipped wheat / barely ankle high, / and sparse as the hair on a dog's belly." Two-and-a-half million people moved out of the Plains states during the Great Depression. Many of these families traveled to California as Livie

Killian's family did. They often found their new lives in California to be just as hard as the ones they had left. They picked crops for very low wages and lived in poor shacks or crowded camps. Families who moved around and did seasonal work like picking crops were called migrants.

The 1930s were especially hard on young adults. They had the greatest difficulty finding work. Times got so tough that at the peak of the Depression, nearly a quarter of a million teenagers were riding the rails. "Riding the rails" means they would stow away on train cars and travel from place to place in search of work, food, or adventure. Many found none of those things. In *Out of the Dust*, Billie Jo rides the rails when she runs away.

By late 1935, when the novel ends, the Depression and the dust storms are still going strong, but Billie Jo is hopeful. "And as long as the / dust doesn't crush / the winter wheat, / we'll have something to show in the spring / for all Daddy's hard work. / Not a lot, but more than last year." Dust Bowl farmers would not have a good crop again until 1939.

Thinking about the setting

- What do you think it was like to live in Oklahoma in the 1930s? What do you think the worst part would be? What would be the best part?
- How would it feel to experience a dust storm? What is the worst storm that you have been through? How do you think a dust storm compares?

"Just as Billie Jo forgave Ma. Just
as Billie Jo forgave Daddy. Just as
Billie Jo forgave herself. And with that
forgiveness Billie Jo finally set her roots
and turned toward her future."

—Karen Hesse, excerpt from Newbery
acceptance speech, June 27, 1998

A novel's themes are its important ideas. *Out of the Dust* has three main themes: forgiveness, healing, and community.

Forgiveness

Sometimes even the people we love can make us angry. Nobody knows that better than Billie Jo Kelby. She adores Ma and always obeys her rules. But there are times when Ma's rules seem unfair. When Ma won't let Billie Jo miss school to play piano, Billie Jo is furious. As soon as Ma's back is turned, Billie Jo gives her a look that is "foul as maggoty stew." Later, when Billie Jo gets a top score on the state tests, Ma doesn't make a fuss. All she says is, "I knew you could." Billie Jo knows Ma is proud but wishes she would show it.

Even though Ma can make Billie Jo angry sometimes, it is nothing like the anger she feels after the fire in the kitchen. Billie Jo is mad at Daddy, at herself, and even at the land. She must learn to forgive before she can find hope and happiness again.

Forgiving family
After Ma and baby Franklin die in the accident, Billie Jo and Daddy are the only ones left in the Kelby home. Instead of helping each other through the very sad time, Billie Jo and her father barely speak. Billie Jo says, "I don't know my father anymore. . . ./I am awkward with him,/and irritated,/and I want to be alone/but I am terrified of being alone."

Billie Jo is full of anger toward her father. She blames him for putting kerosene next to the stove. It was the kerosene that caused the fire that killed Ma. She is also mad at her father for using the family's emergency money to buy drinks at a bar in Guymon while Ma was suffering from her burns.

Billie Jo cannot find it in her heart to forgive her father. She says, "I can almost forgive him the taking of Ma's money,/I can almost forgive him his night in Guymon,/getting drunk./But as long as I live,/no matter how big a hole he digs,/I can't forgive him that pail of kerosene. . . ."

As time passes, Billie Jo's feelings only get stronger. She gets angry with Daddy for not knowing Mad Dog Craddock's real name: "Ma could have told me." She doesn't like Daddy going to night school and "spending time with all those biddies," either. Worst of all, she hates that her father won't respond to Aunt

Ellis's letter. Aunt Ellis wants Billie Jo to live with her in Texas even though Billie Jo doesn't want to go.

Daddy isn't the only person making Billie Jo mad. She is mad at herself, too. She feels guilty about the fire. When the neighbors talk about what happened, Billie Jo gets very upset. "'Billie Jo threw the pail,'/they said. 'An accident,'/they said. /Under their words a finger pointed." Billie Jo is sensitive to what the ladies have to say because she hasn't forgiven herself for what happened to her mother and Franklin—even though it was an accident.

Billie Jo wishes someone were there to take care of her and make her feel better. She longs for her mother. In her longing, she finds a way to understand Ma and forgive her for the times she seemed too tough. Billie Jo explains, ". . . no matter how brittle and sharp she seemed,/she was still my ma who loved me."

Yet nothing can make Billie Jo forgive her father. Billie Jo is so full of sadness and anger that she decides to run away. She says, "I have given my father so many chances/to understand, to/reach out, to/love me."

When Billie Jo runs away, she spends a lot of time thinking about what happened to her family. She even discusses Daddy with a man she meets in a train boxcar. "I told him about my father,/and how the thing that scared us both the most/was being left alone./And now I'd gone and left him." Billie Jo begins to understand that her father had been there for her all along.

"My father / stayed rooted, even with my tests and my temper, / even with the double sorrow of / his grief and my own, / he had kept a home / until I broke it."

Billie Jo decides to return home. When her father meets her at the station, she is able to call him Daddy for the first time since the accident. She is also able to talk to him and share her feelings. As she opens up to Daddy, she begins to forgive him— and herself. "As we walk together, / side by side, / in the swell of dust, / I am forgiving him, step by step, / for the pail of kerosene. / As we walk together, / side by side, / in the sole-deep dust, / I am forgiving myself / for all the rest."

Once Billie Jo forgives herself and her family, she is able to stop living in the sad memories of the past and look to the future with new hope.

Forgiving the land
Sometimes weather can be dangerous and cause great damage. Have you ever had a hurricane, tornado, drought, or blizzard hit your town? These disasters can be so bad that they destroy homes or hurt innocent people. It can make you angry just thinking about it.

Billie Jo and her father are angry about the weather they face. Rain seldom falls. Dust storm follows dust storm. Crops dry up. Cattle grow thin. Many people move away because they can no longer rely on the land to feed their families.

Sometimes, rain or snow falls. One night Billie Jo hears rain falling. "I hear the first drops. / Like the tapping of a stranger / at the door of a dream, / the rain changes everything." But soon the rain is followed by yet another dust storm.

Daddy's wheat crop fails year after year. Each dust storm is harder for Billie Jo to accept. "I can hardly make myself / get started cleaning again." To make things worse, Billie Jo and her father know that people are partly to blame for the problems with the land. Farmers in Oklahoma and nearby states had cleared too much land and planted too much wheat. When the wheat crops began to fail, the topsoil blew away because the farmers had plowed away the sod that had kept the soil in place.

Billie Jo runs away to get "out of the dust." Daddy is so troubled by the land that Billie Jo believes he has given up. He won't even let the doctor treat his skin cancer.

However, just as Billie Jo is able to forgive herself and her family, she and Daddy slowly learn to forgive the land and the dust. The dust storms still strike, but the family has stopped feeling angry and helpless. Instead, they work with the land. Daddy starts using farming practices that help restore and protect the soil. "Daddy said he'd try some sorghum, / maybe some cotton, / admitting as how there might be something / to this notion of diversification folks were / talking about. . . ." Daddy has also started using a pair of mules instead of a tractor. Billie Jo thinks this is a good thing. She explains, "Maybe the tractor lifted him above the land, / maybe the fields didn't know him anymore, / didn't remember the touch of his feet, / or the stroke of his hand, / or the bones of his knees, / and why should wheat grow for a stranger?"

Together, the Kelbys begin to look to the land with hope and not distrust.

Healing

In *Out of the Dust*, Billie Jo and Daddy are both hurting—on the outside and the inside.

Billie Jo burns her hands in a horrible kitchen fire. After she is hurt, she explains that "there are only these / lumps of flesh / that once were hands long enough to span octaves, / swinging at my sides." Daddy is not well, either. He has skin cancer, the kind that killed his own father. "My father has a raised spot / on the side of his nose / that never was there before / and won't go away. / And there's another on his cheek / and two more on his neck, / and I wonder / why the heck is he fooling around. / He knows what it is."

The physical problems Billie Jo and Daddy show on the outside tell us how they are feeling on the inside. After the accident, nothing goes right for Billie Jo. She struggles with the never-ending dust storms, and she feels anger and guilt about Ma's and Franklin's deaths. She and Daddy don't talk much anymore, so she finds no comfort at home. As the pain inside Billie Jo grows, her hands refuse to heal. She can't even play her beloved piano. "I couldn't play. / It had been too long. / My hands wouldn't work. / I just sat on the piano bench, / staring down at the keys." Billie Jo wants her hands to get better but she has lost hope.

Daddy has lost hope, too. His wheat farm is doing badly. His wife and son are gone, and Billie Jo's scarred hands remind him of the accident every day. When Daddy discovers spots on his skin, he knows they are cancer, but he won't see Doc Rice. Billie Jo believes she knows why: "I think / he didn't care much, / if he had some cancer / and took and died. / Figured he'd see Ma then, / he'd see my brother. / It'd be out of his hands. / He'd be out of the dust."

When Billie Jo returns home after running away, things begin to change for the Kelby family. Billie Jo and Daddy are finally able to share their feelings with each other. The pain and sadness they've felt starts to get better.

As they heal on the inside, Billie Jo and Daddy are ready to heal on the outside, too. Billie Jo pleads with Daddy. She wants them both to see Doc Rice. "And I tell him how scared I am / about these spots on / his skin / and I see he's scared too." Daddy agrees to go, and Doc Rice removes the cancerous spots on his skin. "Now he's going to wear bandages / where Doc cut the cancer out / the best he could." Doc also tells Billie Jo her hands will get better. "They'll heal up fine if you just use them." Billie Jo listens to his advice. "And I've / been playing / a half hour / every day, / making the skin stretch, / making the scars stretch." As *Out of the Dust* ends, both Daddy and Billie Jo have begun to heal in every way.

Community

Everyone in Billie Jo's community is poor. Times have been tough since the dust storms began. "We haven't had a good crop in three years, / not since the bounty of '31, / and we're all whittled down to the bone these days. . . ." Even though the characters in *Out of the Dust* are facing hard times, they are willing to help others in their community.

Throughout the novel, we see neighbors reaching out to one another. Billie Jo's family is always willing to give to those who are less fortunate. Ma gladly donates food and a baby nightie to people in the community who need them even though her own family has little to eat and she is expecting a baby. And when a teenage boy comes by the house, he is given food, a bath, a haircut, and clean clothes. Billie Jo shares what she has, too. When she meets a man on a boxcar heading west, she gives him two biscuits. "I'll be hungry tonight, / what with giving my day's biscuits away. / But I can see the gaunt of hunger in his cheeks."

Billie Jo also learns about giving to others at school. Her teacher, Miss Freeland, is very kind to her students. She takes Billie Jo to the Christmas dinner since Billie Jo doesn't have Ma to take her anymore. The school also opens its doors to a migrant family. Students share their food and bring in clothes and toys for the family's children.

Everyone in the community looks out for one another. People come out in support of President Roosevelt's fund-raising balls, and "the whole of Joyce City came forward with gifts" when the reverend took in an abandoned baby. When a terrible dust storm struck during a funeral, Billie Jo and Daddy are welcomed by a kind neighbor. "A woman opened her home to us, / all of us, / not just me and my father, / but the entire funeral procession."

Even those people who receive help want to give back to the community. Buddy Williams, the father of the migrant family staying at the school, helps with repairs and cleans up the schoolyard. The teenage boy who Billie Jo's family helps asks to work for his meal.

A helpful community helps the characters in *Out of the Dust* make it through the difficult years of the Dust Bowl.

Thinking about the themes

- Which of the three themes do you think is the most important? Why?
- Have you ever had to forgive someone? Did forgiving that person make you feel better?
- In what ways do people in your community help one another?

A closer look: Sometimes an author uses repeated images in a novel. These are things that show up again and again as the story unfolds. These images can help an author connect ideas, draw the reader's attention, and add another layer of meaning to the story. Some of the repeated images in *Out of the Dust* are pianos, fire, apples, and babies. Can you find examples of these images? How do you think repeating them adds to the story?

Free Verse: Why Is *Out of the Dust* Written Like That?

"I never attempted to write this book any other way than in free verse."

—Karen Hesse, excerpt from Newbery acceptance speech, June 27, 1998

When you opened *Out of the Dust* for the first time, you probably noticed something unusual. The novel is not written paragraph by paragraph. Instead, it is a series of poems.

The style of poetry used in *Out of the Dust* is called free verse. Free-verse poems don't rhyme. They don't follow a particular rhythm, either. Each line of free verse can be as long or as short as the author wants it to be.

Karen Hesse has explained her decision to use free verse: "I realized [Billie Jo] lived a very spare life. Everything she did was carefully considered, because it took so much to survive, to get through one day living with parents who were struggling. It seemed as if the only way to get at that spareness was to tell it through poetry."

Many book reviewers have praised Karen Hesse for writing *Out of the Dust* in free verse. Because every poem is written from

Billie Jo's point of view, we get to know what it feels like to experience a dust storm or live through a terrible accident. The poetic language used adds to our understanding as well.

Where do I begin?: Tips for reading free verse

Each poem in *Out of the Dust* is written as if it were an entry in Billie Jo's diary. As you read each one, look for the following elements.

Title

Each poem has a title. Sometimes the title summarizes what is being described in the entry. For example, the January 1934 entry called "Permission to Play" is about Billie Jo getting Ma's permission to play piano at the Palace. However, the title may also give you information that isn't found anywhere else. The August 1934 entry titled "Birthday" describes how Billie Jo walks to town and stands outside Arley Wanderdale's house to listen to him play piano. There is no mention of her birthday in the poem. The title is the only way we know that this is how Billie Jo spent her birthday.

Before you begin each entry, read the title. What do you think the entry will be about? After you have finished the entry, read the title again. Did you guess correctly? What does the title tell you?

Word placement

In free verse, words can be placed anywhere on a page. There can be one word per line or dozens of words. Some lines are indented, and others are not. The structure of each line is so meaningful that when poetry is quoted, a slash mark is used to show where each line ends. The following excerpt from "Fields of Flashing Light" looks like this in the novel:

> I sensed it before I knew it was coming.
> I heard it,
> smelled it,
> tasted it.
> Dust.

However, when the excerpt is quoted the lines of verse are separated with slash marks: "I sensed it before I knew it was coming. / I heard it, / smelled it, / tasted it. / Dust."

The author chose the exact location of each word, so pay careful attention to word placement as you read each poem. Is each line long or short, or do the lines vary in length? Short lines draw your attention to each word. The entry called "The Accident" in July 1934 begins with "I got / burned / bad." and ends with "Ma / got / burned / bad." Each line is only a word or two long because each word is very important.

Spacing is an important factor to look at, too. When you read the poem, check to see if the lines are indented or if there are large spaces between words. For example, look at the placement of the words of the entry titled "On Stage" in January 1934:

> When I point my fingers at the keys,
>   the music
> springs straight out of me.

                            Right hand
                playing notes sharp as
                                tongues,
                telling stories while the
                                smooth
                buttery rhythms back me up
                                on the left.

You can almost feel the movement of Billie Jo's hands across the piano as you look at the way the lines are indented.

Repetition

Sometimes words are repeated within a poem. Repetition may highlight an exciting and dramatic moment. The description of a dust storm that happened in March 1934 uses repetition: "The wind snatched that snow right off the fields, / leaving behind a sea of dust, / waves and / waves and / waves of / dust, / rippling across our yard." The repetition of the word *waves* helps us to see and feel the power of the dust storm.

In other cases, words are repeated to help us better understand Billie Jo. When Buddy Williams and his family move into the school in February 1935, Billie Jo describes them as "A man and his wife, pretty far along with a baby / coming, / a baby / coming. . . ." When the phrase "a baby coming" is repeated, it is a clue to us that Billie Jo is thinking about more than just the Williams family. She is probably remembering when her own ma had "a baby coming."

When you read each poem, look for repeated words. Why do you think the author chose to write the poem that way?

Similes and metaphors

The poems in *Out of the Dust* use comparisons called similes and metaphors. Similes are comparisons that use the words *like* or *as*. One example of a simile in *Out of the Dust* is "On Sunday, / winds came, / bringing a red dust, / like prairie fire." The dust is compared to a hot prairie fire, using the word *like*.

Metaphors are similar to similes but do not use *like* or *as*. For example, when Billie Jo describes her ma, she says, "She's an old mule on the subject of my schooling." Billie Jo doesn't mean that Ma is actually a mule. She is just comparing her to one to explain that Ma is stubborn.

Similes and metaphors are tools that writers use to make their writing more colorful. Karen Hesse could have written "the dust was hot." Or "Ma was stubborn." Instead, she chose to use similes and metaphors. This poetic language makes Billie Jo's experiences more interesting and more vivid.

Thinking about free verse

- Do you agree with Karen Hesse's decision to write *Out of the Dust* using free verse? Why or why not?
- Which entry in *Out of the Dust* is your favorite? Why?
- Look for similes and metaphors in the entries in *Out of the Dust*. What do they add to the story?

> "the fact is
> what I am,
> I am because of the dust."
>
> —Billie Jo, *Out of the Dust*

As you read *Out of the Dust*, you will meet many different characters who are part of Billie Jo's family and community. Here is a list of those people. It is followed by brief descriptions of the most important characters.

The Kelby family

Billie Jo Kelby	a thirteen-year-old girl, the book's main character and narrator
Ma ("Pol" Kelby)	Billie Jo's mother
Daddy (Bayard Kelby)	Billie Jo's father
Franklin Kelby	Billie Jo's baby brother
Aunt Ellis	Billie Jo's aunt

People in the community

Coach Albright	the basketball coach at Billie Jo's school
Reverend Bingham	a minister

Mad Dog Craddock	a boy from Billie Jo's school who plays piano and sings
Joe De La Flor	a rancher
Miss Freeland	Billie Jo's teacher
County Agent Dewey	a government worker
Mr. Hardly	a storekeeper
Livie Killian	Billie Jo's friend who moves to California
Louise	Daddy's friend
Mrs. Love	the lady from FERA
Grandma Lucas	an elderly woman who has recently passed away
Doc Rice	a doctor
Miller Rice	a musician
Arley Wanderdale	a music teacher and local musician
Vera Wanderdale	Arley Wanderdale's wife and the person in charge of the dance revue at the Palace Theatre
Buddy Williams	a migrant worker who lives at Billie Jo's school with his family

Billie Jo Kelby: Billie Jo is the main character of the book. She is a thirteen-year-old girl who loves eating apples and playing piano. Tall and thin, Billie Jo has red hair and freckles on her face. She says, "I hollered myself red the day I was born. / Red's the color I've stayed ever since."

Life is hard on Billie Joe and her Oklahoma farming family. Their wheat crop keeps failing and little money is coming in. Even though things have been rough, Billie Jo manages to find happiness as the novel begins. She does well at school and helps Daddy work their farm. She is also looking forward to the arrival of the family's new baby.

Billie Jo is a talented piano player. When Arley Wanderdale offers her the chance to perform at the Palace Theatre, Billie Jo is excited. "How supremely / heaven / playing piano / can be," she says. Shortly before her fourteenth birthday, Billie Jo burns her hands in the accident that kills Ma. Still, she tries to find joy in her music. Arley Wanderdale encourages her to play in the dance revue. She practices every day and wins third prize.

With Ma gone, Billie Jo tries to create a normal life at home for herself and her father. She cooks the meals and tries to clean up the dust the way her mother did. But nothing is normal for Billie Jo. Her life gets harder every day. Dust storms and fire damage her community, and her father is showing signs of skin cancer. To make things worse, she doesn't have anyone to talk to. She feels out of place with her old friends like Mad Dog Craddock, and her hands begin hurting her so badly that she can't even practice the piano anymore. Billie Jo is most upset that her father doesn't talk to her or try to comfort her. Soon she can no longer face her father, her anger, or the dust. So she runs away.

While she's traveling west, Billie Jo shares her life story with a man she meets in a boxcar. She discovers what she has to do to make things right. She must return to her father and tell him how she feels. When she does, she is able to find some happiness once again. She begins to practice piano and declares that she is thankful for "the certainty of home, the one I live in, / and the one / that lives in me."

"Pol" Kelby/Ma: Ma is Billie Jo's strict but caring mother and another main character in the book. Ma is a proud woman. She makes Billie Jo return four cents to Mr. Hardly when he gives her too much change. She also insists on keeping a neat home for her family. She has "rules for dining" that keep the dust out of the food, and she is good at cleaning up after a dust storm. "She never could stand a mess."

Ma is very generous to those in need, but she is more sensible when it comes to her own family. She encourages Daddy to dig a pond, try different crops, and prepare for the fact that it may not rain. She is also saving money to send Billie Jo to college to study music.

Ma appears to have come from a different background than the farming life she married into. Billie Jo says, "I don't think she was ever / really meant for farm life, / I think she once had bigger dreams, / but she made herself over / to fit my father."

Billie Jo says Ma "isn't much to look at." She is tall, thin, and has long, dark hair and bad teeth. Yet Ma tries to surround herself with beautiful things. She has a book of poetry, and she spends lots of time tending to her apple trees until they burst with blossoms. She longs for rain so badly that when a drizzle comes, she stands naked in the rain to enjoy it fully. Ma also plays piano in the family's parlor. Billie Jo explains: "In the kitchen she is my ma, / in the barn and the fields she is my daddy's wife, / but in the parlor Ma is something different." Her piano playing is so dazzling that even a tired Daddy "gets soft eyes" when she plays.

In August 1934, Ma dies from the burns she received in a tragic kitchen fire.

Bayard Kelby/Daddy: Billie Jo's father is another important character in the book. He is a wheat farmer who fought in France during World War I. He is a handsome man "with his strong back, / and his blondy-red hair / and his high cheekbones rugged with wind." He is also a man of few words.

Daddy believes in his land and his crops. His wheat crops have failed three years in a row, but he keeps working the land. He is even willing to take a loan from the government so that he can plant more wheat. He explains, "I can turn the fields over, / start again. / It's sure to rain soon. / Wheat's sure to grow." Even after another dust storm destroys his latest crop, Daddy stubbornly refuses to think about trying to use his land for anything else. "It has to be wheat. / I've grown it before. / I'll grow it again."

After his wife dies in the accident and his wheat is destroyed by grasshoppers, Daddy's hope turns to doubt. He starts digging a hole that is six feet deep. Billie Jo thinks he is building the pond Ma wanted.

By autumn 1934, Daddy is trying to move on with his life. He takes a job as a hired hand at Wireless Power, signs up for night school, and gets another loan to grow wheat. But Daddy is not the same as he was before the accident. He has stopped caring about himself. He has skin cancer, but he won't go see Doc Rice. Daddy is not the same with Billie Jo, either. He hardly talks to his daughter and won't reach out to her even though she is suffering.

After Billie Jo returns from running away and tells her father she is afraid of losing him, Daddy finally agrees to see Doc Rice.

Things start getting better for Daddy. He reaches out to Billie Jo and is happy about his engagement to Louise. He has also learned that he can't be so stubborn about the farm. He decides to plant different kinds of crops.

Louise: Louise is another main character. She is Daddy's teacher at night school. When Billie Jo leaves home, Louise stays with Daddy. By the time Billie Jo returns, Louise has become an important part of Daddy's life. She often comes to the Kelbys' home for dinner.

Soon Louise proves to be a source of hope and comfort for both Billie Jo and Daddy. She's a good listener, and she's able to help Daddy and Billie Jo get along better as a family. But, most of all, Louise "knows how to come into a home / and not step on the toes of a ghost." Louise doesn't try to replace Ma. Instead, she helps the family create new traditions.

It seems that Louise needs the Kelbys, too. She has never been married before "and didn't notice how lonely she was / until she met Daddy and fell into the / big hurt of his eyes."

By the end of the novel, Daddy and Louise are engaged to be married. Although it is December, Louise stops by the Kelby home with a flowered hat "and when she smiles, / her face is / full enough of springtime, it makes / her hat seem just right." Like springtime, Louise provides the Kelby home with a fresh, hopeful new beginning.

Mad Dog Craddock: Mad Dog Craddock is an important character because of his close friendship with Billie Jo. He is blue-eyed, handsome, and popular. He is also a talented singer and piano player. Mad Dog is such a good piano player that Billie Jo is jealous of him. Yet, in spite of her jealousy, it is clear that he is a good friend to Billie Jo. Billie Jo is thankful that he treats her like a regular person after the accident. "He looks at me like I am / someone he knows, / someone named Billie Jo Kelby."

Mad Dog is the opposite of the people who are leaving to escape the dust. He has the talent to leave Oklahoma. He's been performing at a radio station in Amarillo, Texas. Yet he keeps coming back to Oklahoma and the dust. Before he leaves for Amarillo for the first time, he explains, "I love this land, / no matter what." Whenever Mad Dog comes home, he always stops by to see Billie Jo.

Thinking about the characters

- Other than Billie Jo, who do you think is the most memorable character? Explain your answer.
- How has Billie Jo changed by the end of the novel?
- How does Daddy affect how Billie Jo thinks and feels? Do other characters influence one another in similar ways?

What do you write when your assignment is to review *Out of the Dust*? Lots of good things! Ted Hipple from the magazine *The ALAN Review* loved *Out of the Dust* so much that he wrote, "Please read this book." A reviewer from *The Five Owls* magazine called the novel "a literary groundbreaker as stunning as Oklahoma's dust bowl recovery."

What makes *Out of the Dust* so special? Many people point to Billie Jo's character. Ted Hipple called Billie Jo "as memorable a heroine as you will meet in YA [young adult] literature."

Others think it's the use of free-verse poetry that makes *Out of the Dust* stand out. (See page 37 for more information about free verse.) Susan Dove Lempke from the magazine *Booklist* called the use of poetry "a superb choice."

Karen Hesse's descriptions of hardship, sadness, and hope have also won praise. Susan Dove Lempke wrote, "The story is bleak, but Hesse's writing transcends [rises above] the gloom and transforms it into a powerfully compelling tale of a girl with enormous strength, courage, and love."

Out of the Dust didn't just earn good reviews. It won awards, too. Lots of them. Each year, several important groups work hard to create lists of the best books that were published that year. *Out of the Dust* won a place on many of those lists. It was a *Publishers Weekly* Best Book of the Year, a *Booklist* Editors' Choice, and an ALA (American Library Association) Notable Children's Book, to name just a few.

Out of the Dust also won the Scott O'Dell Award for Historical Fiction in 1998. This award is presented to one outstanding work of historical fiction each year. The book that is honored must be set in the "New World" and published in the United States.

Another award won by *Out of the Dust* was HUGE. It's the John Newbery Medal. Look for the gold medal printed on the front of your copy of *Out of the Dust*. The American Library Association awards the Newbery Medal once a year to the author who has made "the most distinguished contribution to American literature for children." The Newbery Medal earned *Out of the Dust* and Karen Hesse a great deal of attention.

Thinking about what others think of *Out of the Dust*

- Do you agree that Billie Jo is a memorable character? How does she compare with the characters in other books you've read?

- One *Out of the Dust* reviewer wrote, "Please read this book." Would you tell a friend to read *Out of the Dust*? Why or why not?

Here are some important words and terms used in *Out of the Dust*. Understanding these words will make it easier to read the novel.

betrothal a mutual promise to marry

CCC Civilian Conservation Corps, a government program started in 1933. It was created to find jobs for young men ages seventeen to twenty-seven. The men worked in national parks and forests for nine months at a time.

Dionne Quintuplets the world's first-known healthy set of quintuplets. The five babies were born in Ontario, Canada, on May 28, 1934, and became world famous. They were taken from their parents and raised by their doctor until 1943, when they were returned to their parents.

diversification a variety of methods, as in planting different crops

divining a technique used to discover something by instinct, magic, or guessing

dunes sand hills made by the wind

dust pneumonia a serious infection of the lungs caused by dust

FERA Federal Emergency Relief Administration, a U.S. government program created to give money to city and state agencies to aid people who needed financial help

festered rotted, showing pus

infantile paralysis polio, an infectious viral disease that attacks the brain and spinal cord. Polio occurs mainly in children. In serious cases, it can cause paralysis. The disease is now easily prevented by a vaccine. Polio is short for poliomyelitis.

maggoty full of maggots, the larvae of certain flies. Maggots are found in decaying animal matter.

migrant to do with someone who moves around doing seasonal work

mottled If something is mottled, it is covered with patches of different colors.

octave the eight-note gap in a musical scale between a note and the next note of the same name above or below it.

parched very dry

rabbit drive In the 1930s, thousands of hungry jackrabbits that couldn't find food in the wild wandered into Dust Bowl towns. They fed on grass and crops. During rabbit drives, rabbits were herded into a fenced area to keep them from causing more damage.

rag a song, usually written in the ragtime style of music

rapscallions rascals

riled annoyed or irritated

sod the top layer of soil and the grass attached to it

union suit a one-piece undergarment once worn by men that is similar to long underwear

whittled reduced bit by bit

writhe to twist and turn around, as in pain

Karen Hesse on Writing

"The thing about writing...until your words become a book you can change them, mold them, shape and reshape them until they look and sound and feel precisely the way you want."

–Karen Hesse, excerpt from *Something About the Author*

Karen Hesse likes routine. She likes it so much that she wakes up at the same time every day—5:00 A.M.! During the week, she heads for her computer to work on her latest book. On the weekends, she answers the mail she receives from her readers around the world.

Even though Hesse tries to write every day, she has admitted that some days are easier than others: "There are times that writing goes so well I feel I have been given a gift. Then there are times it goes so slowly, it feels like torture. But I know that if I stay at the computer—if I keep at it with every word and every image—it will be okay."

Hesse gets the ideas for her books from many sources. Some of her writing is drawn from her own experiences. Her book *Lavender* is based on her relationship with her favorite aunt.

Sometimes, she simply chooses topics that grab her attention.

What's Hesse's secret for writing one great book after another? "I never do anything in halves," she explains. That means careful research and lots of revising. Although Hesse's research always begins at her local library, it has led her to some unusual places. For example, she spent time at a dolphin research facility in Florida while working on *The Music of Dolphins*.

When Hesse sits down to write her books, she doesn't always get it right the first time. "Writing is not easy," she has explained. "I work for long hours and sometimes that work disappoints me and I throw it out and begin again." Hesse won't give up until she has it perfect. She started her book *Letters from Rifka* twenty times before finally finding the right voice for the main character!

Sometimes Hesse uses photographs when she writes. Look at the photo on the front cover of *Out of the Dust*. It is a famous photograph taken in 1936 by a man named Walker Evans. To Hesse, this photo was her character Billie Jo. She kept it by her computer as she wrote *Out of the Dust*. Hesse has shared, "I often keep a photograph in front of me as I'm writing. I look into the eyes of that person, and in my brain there's a constant checking. 'Would you say this? Would you do this?' It keeps the character focused and real."

What does Hesse tell people who want to be writers? "I say go for it! Anyone who wants to write can. The requisites are to read as much as you can, and to write every day.... Use a diary or journal. If you feel that you have something to say, you probably do. Just don't give up."

- **Is this the end?:** The last entry in *Out of the Dust* is dated December 1935. What do you think happens to Billie Jo and her family next? Does Daddy ever harvest a good wheat crop? Does Billie Jo perform in another concert? What happens with Mad Dog's singing career? Write a new entry for *Out of the Dust* dated December 1936.

- **Stormy weather:** You may not know what it's like to be in a dust storm, but chances are you've seen some extreme weather. Has your town ever had a blizzard, drought, tornado, ice storm, heat wave, or hurricane? Write a story about your wildest weather experience.

- **The other side of the story:** The entries in *Out of the Dust* are written by Billie Jo. They help you understand what she saw, felt, and did. What about the other people in the book? Did they experience things differently than Billie Jo? Try writing an entry from another character's point of view.

- **Poetry power:** Write a one-page story about a day in your life. Some topics you could choose are your last birthday, a day out with your best friend, a time you played your favorite sport, or a concert you performed in at school. Now try writing the same event as free-verse poetry. Remember, your poetry doesn't have to rhyme and it doesn't have to follow a pattern. It can be as long or short as you like as long as it describes your day. Compare the two pieces you wrote. How are they alike? How are they different?

• **Can you picture it?:** Find a picture of someone you don't know. Look in a magazine, a newspaper, or ask your parents if you can borrow an old photo. Write a story about the person in the picture.

Activities

• **Sing the blues:** What kind of music did Billie Jo play on her piano? Find out for yourself! Learn one of the songs mentioned in *Out of the Dust*. Choose "My Baby Just Cares for Me" by Gus Kahn and Walter Donaldson or "Bye, Bye, Blackbird" by Ray Henderson and Mort Dixon.

If you love singing the blues, you could also try one of the songs written by Woody Guthrie (1912–1967). Guthrie was a folk musician who was born in Oklahoma—so he knew all about dust. Check out his songs: "Dust Bowl Blues," "Dust Can't Kill Me," or "Blowin' Down This Road (I Ain't Going To Be Treated This Way)." One place you can find these recordings is on Woody Guthrie's CD titled *Dust Bowl Ballads*. Ask for it at your local library or music store.

• **Dear Mr. President:** Billie Jo was very fond of President Franklin Delano Roosevelt. She even named her baby brother after him. What do you think of the current president? Is he doing a good job? Is there something you'd like him to do to make the United States a better place? Let him know. You can e-mail the president at president@whitehouse.gov. You can also send a letter via snail mail. Address your letter to

The White House
1600 Pennsylvania Avenue N.W.
Washington, D.C. 20500

Be sure to include your age in your letter. You might also include your return address so the president can write back!

- **Bake an apple pandowdy:** Billie Jo loves apples, and she knows that one delicious way to enjoy them is a deep-dish dessert called apple pandowdy. If you'd like to try apple pandowdy for yourself, follow the recipe below. Be sure to have an adult assist you.

Ingredients
2 tablespoons butter
⅓ cup shortening (such as Crisco™)
1½ cups brown sugar
½ cup flour
½ teaspoon salt
1 cup water
4 teaspoons cinnamon
5 large apples
1 teaspoon vanilla extract
1 tablespoon cream or milk

Directions
Step one
Preheat oven to 375 degrees.

Step two
In a medium-size saucepan combine: 1 cup brown sugar, ¼ cup flour, ½ teaspoon salt, 1 cup water, and 1 teaspoon cinnamon. Place over low heat and stir periodically with a wooden spoon until the mixture thickens (this takes about 10 to 15 minutes).

Remove from heat and add 2 teaspoons cinnamon, 2 tablespoons butter, and 1 teaspoon vanilla extract. Stir together. Cover and set aside.

Step three
Peel the skin off of the five apples. Slice the apples and discard the cores. Place the sliced apples into a greased 9-inch-square baking dish.

Step four
Using a potato masher or fork, combine ⅓ cup shortening, ¼ cup flour, ½ cup brown sugar, and 1 teaspoon cinnamon in a medium-size bowl. Mash the ingredients together until they look like lumpy oatmeal. Mix in 1 tablespoon cream or milk.

Step five
Pour the mixture from step two on top of the apples. Spoon the mixture from step four on top of the apples, trying to spread the mixture evenly over the apples. Bake at 375 degrees for 30 minutes. With an adult's help, remove from oven, let cool, and serve with vanilla ice cream.

• **Keep a journal:** Remember the events in your life by keeping a journal like Billie Jo did. Think about what details someone might find interesting seventy-five or one hundred years from now. What is going on in the news? Who is president? What is your home like? What kind of clothing do you wear? What music do you listen to? What activities are you involved in? Don't forget to put the date before each entry.

• **Get the real story:** If you'd like to find out more about life during the Depression, ask an older relative or neighbor if you can interview them about their experiences during the 1930s. Be sure to bring a pen and paper, a laptop, or a tape recorder so you can record what is said. Before you do your interview, think of what questions you'd like to ask. Some possibilities include: How old were you during the Depression? Where did you live? How did your family earn money during the Depression? What did you think of President Franklin Roosevelt? Did you ever experience a dust storm? Do you remember hearing about the dust storms? Make sure to thank the person you interview.

• **Map it!:** The places discussed in *Out of the Dust* are real. Try finding the following sites on a map of Oklahoma: Keyes, Guymon, Texhoma, Goodwell, Felt, Cimarron River, Beaver River, Black Mesa.

• **Dig up the past:** Billie Jo talks about the dinosaur bones that were found near her home. Cimarron County, Oklahoma, was a very popular spot for dinosaurs that lived millions of years ago. Dinosaurs loved the hot, humid weather, the beach, and the cypress trees that existed in Cimarron County in prehistoric times.

Oklahoma isn't the only place dinosaurs roamed. Dinosaurs lived throughout North America. A few probably even lived in your neighborhood. If you do a little research, you can discover which prehistoric creatures called your town home. One place to start is the Discovery Channel's Web site. Go to: http://dsc.discovery. com/convergence/dinos/lookup.html. Just type in your zip code to find the names of the dinosaurs that lived near you.

Related Reading

Other books by Karen Hesse

Come On, Rain! (1998) (illustrated by Jon J. Muth)

Just Juice (1999)

Lavender (1993)

Lester's Dog (1993) (illustrated by Nancy Carpenter)

Letters from Rifka (1992)

A Light in the Storm: The Civil War Diary of Amelia Martin, Fenwick Island, Delaware, 1861 (1999) (Dear America series)

The Music of Dolphins (1996)

Phoenix Rising (1994)

Poppy's Chair (1993) (illustrated by Kay Life)

Sable (1994) (illustrated by Marcia Sewell)

Stowaway (2000) (illustrated by Robert Andrew Parker)

A Time of Angels (1995)

Wish on a Unicorn (1991)

Witness (2001)

Books with contributions by Karen Hesse

A Christmas Carol (2000) by Charles Dickens (introduction by Karen Hesse)

When I Was Your Age: Original Stories About Growing Up, Vol. 2 (1999), edited by Amy Ehrlich (Karen Hesse is a contributor to the collection.)

Books about the Dust Bowl and the Great Depression—fiction

Angels in the Dust by Roger Essley

Blue Willow by Doris Gates

Bud, Not Buddy by Christopher Paul Curtis

Cat Running by Zilpha Keatley Snyder

Esperanza Rising by Pam Muñoz Ryan

Ida Early Comes Over the Mountain by Robert Burch

The Journal of C. J. Jackson: A Dust Bowl Migrant (My Name Is America series) by William Durbin

A Long Way from Chicago by Richard Peck

Purely Rosie Pearl by Patricia A. Cochrane

Red-Dirt Jessie by Anna Myers

Roll of Thunder, Hear My Cry by Mildred D. Taylor

Survival in the Storm: The Dust Bowl Diary of Grace Edwards (Dear America series) by Katelan Janke

Treasures in the Dust by Tracy Porter

A Year Down Yonder by Richard Peck

Books about the Dust Bowl and the Great Depression—nonfiction

Children of the Dust Bowl: The True Story of the School at Weedpatch Camp by Jerry Stanley

Driven from the Land: The Story of the Dust Bowl (Great Journeys series) by Milton Meltzer

The Dust Bowl: Disaster on the Plains by Tricia Andryszewski

Six Days in October: The Stock Market Crash of 1929 by Karen Blumenthal

This Land Was Made for You and Me: The Life and Songs of Woody Guthrie by Elizabeth Partridge

Woody Guthrie: Poet of the People by Bonnie Christensen

Bibliography

Books

Hedblad, Alan, ed. *Something About the Author.* Volume 103.
Farmington Mills, Mich.: The Gale Group, Inc., 1999.

Hesse, Karen. Essay in *Something About the Author.* Volume 113.
Farmington Mills, Mich.: The Gale Group, Inc., 2000.

Rockman, Connie, ed. "Hesse, Karen." *Eighth Book of Junior
Authors and Illustrators.* Bronx, N.Y.: H.W. Wilson, 2000.

Scholastic Children's Dictionary. New York, N.Y.: Scholastic Inc.,
2002.

Reviews and magazine articles

Beck, Cathy, Linda Gwyn, Dick Koblitz, Anne O'Connor, Kathryn
Mitchell Pierce, and Susan Wolf, "Talking About Books: Karen
Hesse," *Language Arts*, January 1999. Volume 76, Number 3,
pp. 263–271.

Devereaux, Elizabeth, "Karen Hesse: A Poetics of Perfection,"
Publishers Weekly, February 8, 1999, pp. 190–191.

Hendershot, Judy and Jackie Peck, "Newbery Medal Winner
Karen Hesse Brings Billie Jo's Voice Out of the Dust," *The
Reading Teacher*, May 1999. Volume 52, Issue. 8, pp. 856–858.

Hipple, Ted, review of *Out of the Dust*, ALAN Review, Spring 1998.
Volume 25, Number 3, p. 50.

Katz, Claudia Anne and Sue Ann Kuby, "Inspiration in the Dust,"
Booklinks, April/May 2001. Volume 10, Number 5.

Lempke, Susan Dove, review of *Out of the Dust*, *Booklist*, October 1, 1997, p. 330.

Owens, Thomas S., review of *Out of the Dust*, *Five Owls*, January–February 1998, pp. 60–61.

Publishers Weekly, August 25, 1997, pp. 72–73.

Web sites

The American Experience, Surviving the Dust Bowl:
www.pbs.org/wgbh/amex/dustbowl

The Children's Literature Comprehensive Database:
www.childrenslit.com

Cimarron County Chamber of Commerce:
www.ccccok.org

The Civilian Conservation Corps and the National Park Service, 1933–1942:
www.cr.nps.gov/history/online_books/ccc/ccc1a.htm

Dionne Quintuplets:
http://schwinger.harvard.edu/~terning/bios/Dionne.html

"Dust Bowl." *Grolier Multimedia Encyclopedia.* Grolier, Inc., 2002.
http://gme.grolier.com (November 12, 2002).

Scholastic Inc.:
www.scholastic.com/authorsandbooks

Videos

Surviving the Dust Bowl: The American Experience (PBS Home Video, 1998).